The General Care and Maintenance of

Green Anoles

Including notes on other anoles & vivarium design

by Philippe de Vosjoli

Table of Contents

Introduction

For many of us who have become specialists in herpetoculture, green anoles have become such common pet trade fare that we barely notice them either in stores or in individual collections. Indeed, these neat little lizards have in their own way become the reptilian counterpart of the comet goldfish of the aquarium trade; the inexpensive first reptile that we buy our children when they persist about wanting to own a pet. Many of us tend to forget that green anoles often provided our very first introduction to the class Reptilia and to reptilian consciousness. When we were children, something about that small lizard with those intense little black eyes was totally endearing and captivating, particularly when associated with a story about how "chameleons" can change color. Of course, for children, one of the great features of anoles has always been that they are so tiny and harmless in appearance that parents who would categorically refuse to allow their children to keep a snake or larger lizard will usually give in to buying them a green anole. After that first step, it will usually be quite a bit easier to convince parents to let you keep another kind of reptile. This is the stepping stone strategy to becoming a herpetoculturist.

Until relatively recently, green anoles have suffered from the cheap pet stigma. Just like comet goldfish, green anoles have frequently been marketed as creatures that would survive in inexpensive set-ups such as the pet trade's version of the goldfish bowl for lizards, the mini plastic terrarium. As for food, many pet store owners used to simply state that a few mealworms offered twice a week would keep the little buggers alive. All of this misinformation on anole care was in line with an antiquated pet marketing philosophy that preyed on the fact that many parents and children wouldn't give much thought to spending ten or fifteen dollars for a cheap pet and its set-up. If the animal died, it could be replaced for another couple of bucks. Fortunately, the current trend among pet stores and reptile dealers is to advocate a more responsible philosophy of reptile care away from the disposable animal/cheap set-up, quick sales strategies that once used to be so widespread.

This booklet will present herpetocultural guidelines in line with the current philosophical trend towards responsible herpetoculture. The result, as I hope will be demonstrated by the information and photographs gathered for this booklet, will be an enlightening glimpse into a dimension of the natural world where reptiles still rule: enacting ritual battles for territory, overpowering prey and casting dragon spells that will entrap careless humans into a sense of fascination.

General Information

What's in a name: The correct popular name for the "American chameleon" of the pet trade is green anole. All anoles are members of the genus *Anolis* of which there are more than 200 species. *Anolis* are now considered to be in the New World family Polychridae. The true chameleons are Old World lizards that belong to the family Chameleontidae.

Scientific name: The scientific name of the green anole is *Anolis carolinensis*.

Distribution: This is the only species of anole native to the mainland United States. All other anole species found in south Florida were introduced. The green anole is found from N. Carolina south to Key West and west to southeast Oklahoma and central Texas. It has been introduced in several areas including Hawaii.

Size: The total length of adults will range from 5-8 inches (13-20.3 cm), but only males are likely to exceed 6 inches. The tail will account for nearly two thirds of the total length. Hatchlings have a total length of 2 1/16 to 2 5/8 inches (5.3-6.7 cm).

Dewlaps: These are sometimes also called throat fans. During territorial displays, males will perform brief, repeated extensions of the dewlaps. In most green anoles sold in the pet trade, which frequently originate from Louisiana, the dewlaps are usually pink. In green anoles from south Florida, the dewlaps may vary from whites to pinks to pastel blues and purples.

Sexing: Male anoles eventually grow larger than females. The heads of males become proportionately larger with age. Males have much larger dewlaps compared to females. Most females retain a white to grayish middorsal line more prominent than when present in males (most males lack a middorsal line). If in doubt, the most noticeable difference is the prominent hemipenile bulge clearly visible in older males at the base of the tail.

Growth: Green anoles, if maintained properly, will grow from hatchling to small adult size in 6-8 months.

Longevity: In the wild, green anoles typically live under two and a half years. In captivity, when properly cared for, green anoles have lived up to eight years though typical lifespan is 3-6 years. Unfortunately, many anoles sold in the pet trade seldom live for more than a year because they are generally miscared for and neglected.

A male and female green anole. Notice the dewlap of the displaying male and the whitish middorsal line of the female. Photo by Chris Estep.

A male brown anole (*Anolis sagrei*) displaying its dewlap. This species is readily available in the trade and can be kept with green anoles. Photo by Jim Bridges©.

A six foot long naturalistic vivarium designed by Susan Jones and Vern French, former owners of the famous and now defunct Small Worlds Vivarium in New York, a store which in the 1970's pioneered naturalistic vivarium designs. Photo by Vern French.

A close-up of the left section of the vivarium showing various bromeliads, rosary vine and a number of anole species. The vivarium was lit by a bank of four six foot Vita Lite® bulbs and two small incandescent spotlights. Photo by Vern French.

Morphs: Occasionally, pastel blue specimens of green anoles are collected and offered in the trade. These blue anoles, which are apparently axanthic animals (lacking yellow pigment), are few and far between. According to an anole distributor in Louisiana, one blue anole is brought in by collectors per at least 20,000 specimens. With some efforts in selective breeding, more specimens could become available in the future. As could be expected, these blue anoles fetch high prices, often $100.00 or more at the retail level. Other color mutations are occasionally found in green anoles but few are as attractive as the pastel blue.

Color change: There is a popular misconception that anoles change color to match their surroundings. In fact, these lizards have a rather limited repertoire of color change and from little to none involving pattern change. The most remarkable color changes in vertebrates occur in some of the true chameleons, some of which rank among the most beautiful of all the animals. Anoles will change coloration to thermoregulate becoming darker when they are cold and lighter when they are too warm. They also change color as a means to express emotion, such as during territorial displays. At night when sleeping, green anoles adopt a light nocturnal coloration. This color change makes them easily visible when collecting this species with the aid of a flashlight.

SELECTING HEALTHY GREEN ANOLES

The selection of initially healthy animals will be critical to the long term success of maintaining green anoles in captivity.

The following are guidelines which will help you select potentially healthy animals:

1) Select animals that are of small to medium size. Avoid very large animals, as they may be old. Older animals may also be heavily parasitized. They often do not acclimate as well to captivity.

2) Select animals with rounded bodies and rounded tails. Avoid animals in which the hip bones or vertebral processes are prominent and clearly visible through the skin.

3) The eyes of healthy anoles are alert and rounded. Avoid animals with sunken and/or half-closed eyes.

4) Select animals that are active. The "lazy" anole that just sits there in your hand, appearing nearly tame, is probably sick and incapable of behaving like a healthy anole.

5) While holding the animal in your hand, turn it upside down and inspect the vent (opening to the cloaca) and check for smeared watery stools or dried diarrhea. Avoid animals with these symptoms.

6) Don't think for a second you will be able to save the poor sick anole in a store. Sick anoles usually die.

ON KEEPING ANOLE GROUPS

As a general rule, it is recommended to keep anoles either singly or in groups consisting of one male and one or more females but this is a broad guideline. When green anoles are kept under proper conditions where they are not overcrowded, males kept together will establish territories, will demonstrate territorial displays and chase or fight each other, particularly during the breeding season. At that time, weaker males may get injured. There will also be competition during feeding and smaller, weaker animals will be intimidated by larger ones. Whether mixing groups of several males and females will work in the long run will depend on a number of factors including the type of anole species, the number of anoles kept together, the size of the vivarium and the design and landscaping of the vivarium. For example, in the overcrowded conditions in which anoles are maintained at large scale animal dealers, there usually aren't the conditions that allow for the establishment of territories and serious fights are minimal. When keeping anoles in a home vivarium, breaking up the space in a vivarium with tall plants or rocks and wood can allow for enough visual isolation between males that with certain species several can safely be kept together. This is an area where one will have to experiment with respective species.

Inside the screenhouse of a Louisiana green anole distributor. Many large distributors make concerned efforts to provide adequate conditions for their animals. Photo by Terry Stevens.

A naturalistic tropical vivarium designed by the author and Eric Suchman for the Forgotten Forest. Photo by Eric Suchman.

A pothos plant will add a great deal of appeal to an anole setup, even in a simply designed ten gallon vivarium.

Housing and Maintenance

ENCLOSURES

Popular enclosures marketed for keeping green anoles are relatively small plastic terraria with plastic lids. These plastic terraria are useful for the maintenance of a number of other animals but they are inadequate and unsuitable for the long term maintenance of green anoles. Over a period of a few weeks or months, the great majority of anoles kept in these containers die. Keeping anoles in these enclosures is tantamount to keeping a dog in a small kennel with little light, inadequate heat and inadequate stimulation. The new larger versions of plastic terraria (10 gallon or more), provide adequate space but the plastic molded tops create problems in terms of being able to safely provide adequate heat and light. An incandescent bulb in a metal reflector can melt the top. Any herpetoculturist who cared about the welfare of these lizards would not keep them in the mini plastic terraria so frequently recommended in the pet trade.

THE RIGHT KIND OF ENCLOSURES

The best enclosures for keeping green anoles are all-glass tanks with a screen top.

Enclosure size: The minimum size for keeping one to two green anoles should be a standard ten gallon aquarium/vivarium (20"L x 12"H x 10"W) with a standard twenty gallon high (24"W x 16"H x 12"W) being even more desirable. If more than a trio of these animals is to be kept together then a larger size is recommended. If you want to keep several anoles or a variety of plant and animal life, then bigger is better. The best vivaria that the author has seen for anoles were 100 gallon all glass tanks with screen tops six feet long. One of these contained a fascinating array of plant and animal life including five species of lizards, three species of frogs and one species of newt. A well designed vivarium can be as attractive and as captivating as a tropical fish aquarium.

Screen cover: Any enclosure for keeping green anoles should have a secure fitting screen cover. Green anoles can climb glass and will readily escape from any uncovered enclosure.

Designing a Basic Vivarium for Green Anoles

For many people, green anoles will simply be a cheap pet for the children, and they will be unwilling to spend the money required for the design of a naturalistic vivarium. Whatever the case, it will cost several times the price of an anole to purchase even the minimum amount of supplies for successful long term maintenance. In this sense, the keeping of lizards in a vivarium is no different than the keeping of tropical fish where the basic cost of an aquarium exceeds many times over the cost of most fish.

The following are the minimum design requirements for a basic vivarium for the maintenance of green anoles:

MINIMUM REQUIREMENT SET-UPS

Minimum enclosure: A ten gallon all-glass tank with screen top.

Ground medium: An attractive ground medium is seedling or small grade orchid bark. This will be sold by specialist reptile stores or nurseries. Many pet stores will recommend a smooth aquarium pea gravel which will also work. However, sand should not be used as a ground medium. A barely moistened peat moss based potting soil without perlite is also highly recommended for keeping anoles.

Landscaping: Anoles are arboreal (tree dwelling or shrub dwelling) to semi-arboreal lizards which will require suitable climbing areas. To accommodate these behaviors, some branches of select wood with diameters equal to or slightly greater than the width of your lizards should be placed diagonally across the vivarium. Thin pieces of cork bark placed diagonally across the vivarium will also work well. A pot of pothos vine (*Scindapsus aureus* obtainable in most nurseries, plant stores or plant sections in supermarkets) either growing in soil or growing hydroponically in a jar of water should be included and some of the stems spread onto the branches. The leaves of the plant will provide a surface on which anoles can climb and from which they can drink droplets of water. The plant will also help raise the relative humidity in the vivarium.

Lighting: An incandescent bulb in a reflector type fixture should be placed at one end of the vivarium to provide heat. The wattage of bulb required will depend on the air temperature of the room where the vivarium is maintained. For a ten gallon vivarium a 40 to 60 watt bulb is usually adequate for an enclosure with an uncovered screen top maintained at a room temperature of 70°F-74°F. Enclosures which have a partially covered top, either with glass or plexiglas, will require a

lower wattage bulb or the vivarium will overheat. A thermometer should always be used to determine and to help adjust the vivarium temperature. It should read 85°F-90°F when measured at the level of the branches closest to the light. At ground level at the distance furthest from the lights, the temperature should be considerably cooler. Do not place an incandescent bulb directly over live plants or you will stand a good chance of burning the leaves.
Note: A spotlight in a reflector over a smaller vivarium will not allow for a range of heat gradients and will overheat reptiles.

Vitamin/mineral supplements: A good quality powdered reptile or bird multi-vitamin/mineral supplement will be essential for the long term maintenance of your animals and must not be neglected.

A hand sprayer: Use purified water in a hand sprayer to mist plant leaves and the walls of the tank daily. If you simply use regular tap water, you will probably end up with hard to remove and unsightly mineral deposits on the sides of your tank as well as on the leaves of plants.

NOTE: The above are the minimum requirements for maintaining green anoles. For maintaining the other species of amphibians and reptiles compatible with green anoles, a larger enclosure and additional heat in the form of a subtank heater should be included. For most companion species, a shallow water container will have to be included.

Plastic-coated wire mesh cages can be used for displaying large numbers of green anoles in stores. Care must be given to provide adequate humidity through misting and providing of plants.

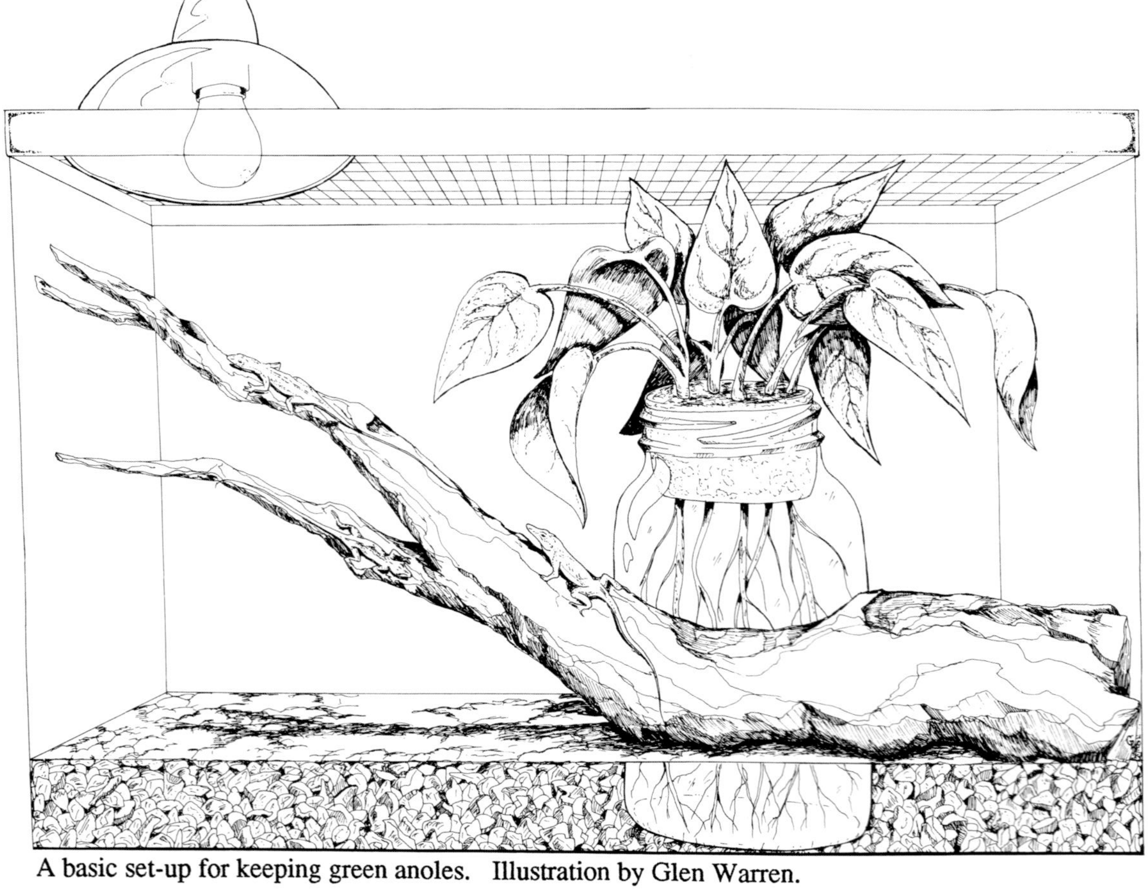

A basic set-up for keeping green anoles. Illustration by Glen Warren.

Designing a Naturalistic Vivarium

The most attractive and interesting vivaria for keeping small reptiles and amphibians are naturalistic vivaria which simulate essential aspects of an animal's habitat in combination with a varied landscape design and a variety of ornamental plants. When planning the design of these vivaria, as much emphasis is placed on the plant species and landscape features as on the species of animals selected. The end result can be vivaria whose aesthetic impact will equal that of the best designed tropical fish aquaria.

The minimum enclosure size for creating a naturalistic vivarium is a standard 20 gallon tank though larger sizes are preferable. As a general rule, the larger the vivarium, the greater the possibilities of incorporating a varied and interesting design.

GROUND MEDIUM

At least two layers of substrata will be required when designing a naturalistic vivarium. On the bottom of the vivarium, a 1-1 1/2 inch layer of coarse gravel should be placed as a drainage layer. Above that, a 2-3 inch layer of a sandy (add 10% sand) peat based potting soil should be placed. Herpetoculturists will often mix in about 10% seedling orchid bark to increase drainage. Do not use commercial potting soils that contain perlite or polystyrene foam. The latter will rise to the surface when the soil is watered and can be ingested by lizards. In addition some herpetoculturists will place after planting and landscaping the vivarium, a layer of small grade orchid bark on parts of the surface of the vivarium. The end result when viewed from the side is a two or three layered substratum. When watered, one will clearly be able to determine whether the soil has been suitably watered or not. As the soil dries out, the moisture level seen from the side will diminish from the top of the soil down. If too much water was applied, the excess water will be seen accumulating in the drainage layer.

LANDSCAPING

As with tropical fish tanks, interesting vivaria are those which have a varied topography. This can be designed by using rocks or driftwood to create layers within the vivarium. Other materials that work are pieces of cork or dried out stumps with root bases emerging from the bottom.

VIVARIUM ALTERNATIVES

Custom-made screen or small wire mesh cages can be practical for stores wishing to keep large numbers of anoles on hand. Branches and a few potted plants will provide all the basic landscaping necessary. Screened cages can also be used by individuals but some visibility will be lost as well as a great deal of display appeal. Extra care will also have to be given to ensure adequate relative humidity. The use of live plants and misting several times a day is recommended.

PLANTS FOR ANOLE VIVARIA

One cannot readily appreciate the behaviors of green anoles without providing plants on which the animals can display their relatively wide range of behaviors. One of the most easily maintained and recommended of vivarium plants is pothos. This popular houseplant can be grown in the vivarium in two ways: hydroponically in a concealed jar of water or planted directly in the ground medium. To grow pothos hydroponically, carefully remove a rooted section of pothos from a pot and rinse the roots of all soil. Then place the section(s), roots first, in a jar of water. Cover the opening with a section of foam rubber. In time, the pothos will form water roots adapted to growing in water. An alternative to using sections with roots is to use stem cuttings. They too will produce water roots in due time.

Other plants that work well in anole vivaria are as follows:

Snakeplants: *Sansevieria sp.* Good choices are:
The birdsnest sansevieria (*Sansevieria t. "Hahnii"*)
The common snakeplant (*Sansevieria t. trifasciata*)
Sansevieria "Moonshine"
Sansevieria metallica. This species has beautiful leaves and is obtainable by mail order from nurseries that specialize in succulents.

There are many other species of suitable sansevierias several of which have odd shaped, cylindrical, and grooved leaves. Their hardiness and unusual forms and patterns make them among the most interesting plants for herpetoculturists, but finding the odd species will take some work such as looking in horticulture magazines and writing specialized succulent nurseries for their catalogs.

Bromeliads:
Many species of bromeliads (members of the pineapple family) will do well in a vivarium with moderately good light (at least two fluorescent bulbs no more than 16 inches from the leaf surfaces) and good drainage (up to 20% orchid bark in the soil medium). Good choices are neoregelias, guzmanias, vriesias and at ground level the various earth stars (*Cryptanthus sp.*). Some of the cultivars such as *Cryptanthus* "It" and species such as *Cryptanthus zonatus* can add beautiful color and patterning in the landscaping of the vivarium. In a large vivarium with banks of 4 fluorescent bulbs or more, some of the epiphytic tillandsias can be grown on

cork bark placed in close proximity to the lights. As a general rule, bromeliads with spiny leaf edges should not be used with amphibians and reptiles because of the possible risks of injuries.

Orchids:
A good candidate for larger tropical vivaria with good drainage and adequate lighting is the terrestrial jewel orchid (*Haemaria discolor*) with beautiful velvety maroon leaves streaked in gold. Moth orchids (*Phalaenopsis*), Dendrobiums and Epidendrums as well as a variety of small epiphytic orchids can be grown in an anole vivarium. Moth orchids or other orchids that are grown in pots are best placed in their pots within the vivarium. The pot can be buried in the substratum or concealed with sections of wood or stone. Epiphytic orchids should be attached to cork bark or wood at a close distance from fluorescent full spectrum lights. There's lots of room for experimentation here and many possible species of orchids to choose from.

Vines:
With good lighting and good drainage, the rosary vine (*Ceropegia woodii*) will grow well and can be sprawled across branches for an attractive effect. In larger vivaria, one can use smaller species of philodendron such as the popular heartleaf philodendron (*Philodendron cordatum*). As a ground cover, creeping fig (*Ficus pumila*) can be used but regular pruning must be practiced or it will become too dense and problematical. With good lighting, many other vines can be successfully grown in the vivarium including other philodendrons, passion vines, odd morning glories and grape relatives.

All of the above mentioned plants have been tested by the author over several years with anoles and will survive in vivaria that include strong light, moderately high relative humidity and adequate ventilation.

HEATING, LIGHTING AND VENTILATION

In tropical vivaria two types of heating should be provided.

1) A below ground or subtank heating system such as nursery soil heating cables or one of the subtank heating devices currently available in the reptile trade. With the use of a rheostat, some of the subtank heating devices sold by reptile dealers can even be adjusted. Care must be taken however to abide by the manufacturer's instructions as to the safe use of these devices to prevent the risk of fire or the cracking of the bottom of one's glass enclosure.

2) Incandescent bulbs or small spotlights should be placed over select basking areas such as sections of cork bark or branches, such that the temperature measures 85°F-90°F at the basking areas closest to the basking light. The wattage required will depend on the size of the enclosure and the distance from basking sites. The

daytime air temperature in the vivarium at the furthest end from the basking sites should be 75°F-84°F.

TEMPERATURE

At least one thermometer should be placed in the vivarium preferably near a basking site. One of the best thermometers for these vivaria are the digital readout thermometers with an outdoor sensor which are sold in most electronic supply stores. These thermometers will allow for a continuous readout from a specific location in the vivarium. With the flick of a switch you can also obtain a reading from the probe, i.e. the basking site. For green anoles, daytime air temperatures in the vivarium should be 75°F-82°F. The temperature at basking sites closest to incandescent bulbs or spotlights should be 85°F-90°F. At night, the temperature can safely drop into the upper 60's and even considerably cooler in the winter (see Breeding). For tropical anoles, the night temperature should not drop below 72°F.

OTHER TYPES OF LIGHTING

For the welfare of plants and the psychological welfare of the animals, full-spectrum fluorescent bulbs such as Vita Lite ® should be placed running the length of the vivarium. Ideally, at least two bulbs should be used. In large vivaria and depending on the plants used, some herpetoculturists will use banks of four bulbs. These bulbs are the key to maintaining attractive naturalistic vivaria. They will provide the lighting that will make plants thrive and orchids bloom. For many lizards the UV-A (a lower frequency of ultraviolet radiation) generated by these bulbs will have psychological benefits that will increase the probability of long term survival and possibly stimulate feeding and breeding.

PHOTOPERIOD

During most of the year, the lights should be set on a timer so that they will remain on 14 hours a day. In the winter the light schedule should be cut back to 10 hours a day particularly if you are interested in breeding the animals. Use a plug in timer.

RELATIVE HUMIDITY

Anoles fare best in vivaria with moderate to high relative humidity 50% or greater (certain tropical species may require at least 80% to fare well). If live plants are maintained in the vivarium and with regular daily misting, these humidity levels can be readily achieved. However, in unusually dry climates, partial covering of the vivarium screen cover with a section of clear plexiglas may be necessary to raise humidity. A small cool air humidifier in a room will also be useful particularly if one is maintaining several vivaria in the same room. See next section for more information.

An elaborate set-up containing rare, exotic plants, a miniature filtered waterfall and various polychrid species including prehensile tailed polychrus (*Polychrus marmoratus*). Photo by Eric Suchman.

A close-up of the bamboo miniature waterfall designed by the author and Eric Suchman for the Forgotten Forest. The inside of the bamboo must be coated with an epoxy paint safe for use with aquatic animals or the bamboo will eventually rot. Photo by Eric Suchman.

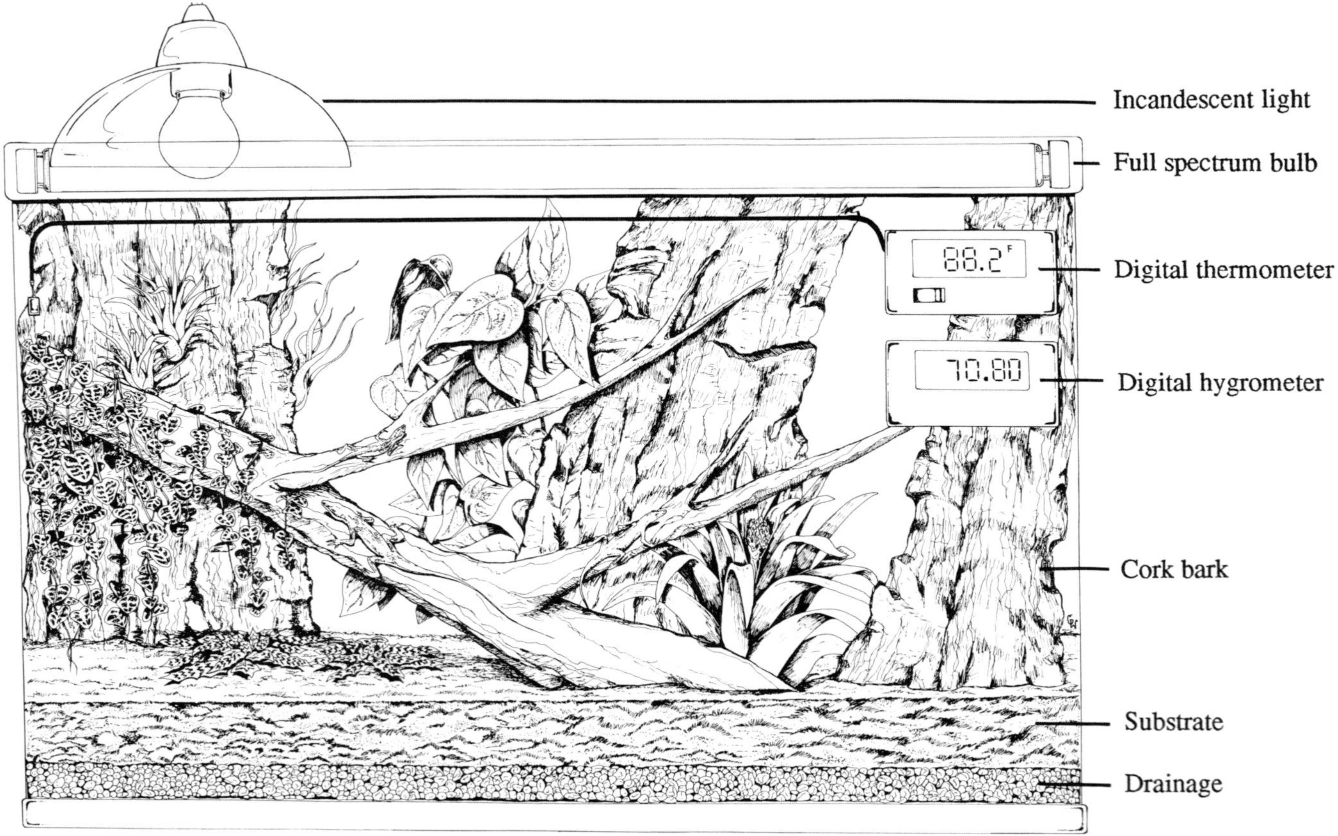
88.2°F
70.80
Incandescent light
Full spectrum bulb
Digital thermometer
Digital hygrometer
Cork bark
Substrate
Drainage

A naturalistic vivarium for anoles. Illustration by Glen Warren.

VENTILATION

In any vivarium containing green anoles or any of the other animals mentioned at the end of this book it is essential that the vivarium have good ventilation. Most amphibians and reptiles (there are a few exceptions) will eventually die if maintained in a mostly covered vivarium with poor ventilation, saturated air humidity and high condensation levels. To successfully maintain anoles and other animals in this type of setup, the screen top should be uncovered with no obstacle to air flow. Only in unusually dry climates should a small section of the screen top (less than 1/3 of the cover surface) be covered to reduce the evaporation rate within the vivarium. Under most circumstances, with daily misting and regular watering, adequate relative air humidity will be easily maintained within the vivarium.

An anole lying on a clump of rosary vine (*Ceropegia woodii*). This succulent species will fare well if provided with a well drained growing medium and strong lights. Photo by Vern French.

Green anoles in a specialized reptile store rushing to grab supplemented 2-3 week old crickets placed in a plastic deli container to reduce dispersal rate. Photo by Chris Estep.

An economical way to supplement the diet of green anoles maintained in large numbers (i.e. animal wholesalers) is to introduce peach baby food supplemented with a vitamin/mineral powder. Photo by Chris Estep.

Anolis tropidonotus from Honduras. As with most anoles, the male (above) is larger than the female (below). Photo by Jim Bridges©.

Feeding

FOOD SELECTION AND SIZE

The most readily available and most recommended food for green anoles are commercially raised crickets. For adult *A. carolinensis* two to three week old crickets are recommended. Many pet stores sell 5-6 week old crickets that are too large for this species. Mealworms are not a recommended food for green anoles unless one raises these worms at home, in which case smaller mealworms 1\16 of an inch thick can be used but only as an occasional component of the diet. However, just molted "white" mealworms with a soft exoskeleton are also a suitable food for adults of these lizards. The problem with standard mealworms is that their chitinous exoskeleton is undigestible and also too thick for anoles to readily tear while chewing. A common occurrence is for anoles to grab and swallow a whole large mealworm only to regurgitate it a day or two later. If you really care, you will buy the right size crickets to feed your anoles. In small quantities to diversify the diet, small wax worms, the caterpillars of the wax moth (*Galleria mellonella*,) are recommended. If the caterpillars are allowed to pupate (which they will if maintained at warmer temperatures), the resulting moths will be relished by anoles.

A favorite food of anoles are flies which can be offered for variety but should never make up their primary diet unless you want to gut load the flies on a nutritious diet such as moist dog food or lean meat with multivitamins. To obtain flies the best source are the commercially bred fly larvae (now available in many specialized reptile stores) raised on a relatively hygienic vegetarian diet such as corn meal. At warm temperatures, the larvae will pupate. The pupae can then be placed in a small container inside the vivarium, and the flies allowed to emerge.

FOOD PREPARATION

Commercially-raised insects tend to lose weight as well as nutritional value during shipping and during storage in a pet store. In addition, the nutritional quality of diets fed to crickets is often inadequate to provide proper nutrition to reptiles (see De Vosjoli 1991). Indeed a significant amount of the nutritional qualities of insects are the result of dietary matter stored in their guts.

Thus, crickets and mealworms prior to feeding to green anoles should first be nutrient loaded. This is done by placing the crickets for 12-24 hours in a small plastic terrarium and offering them either chicken mash or ground rodent chow or high quality tropical fish flakes or high protein flaked baby cereal. As a source of water and vitamin C, offer the crickets slices of orange. As a source of beta-carotene, alternate with some grated carrots. Offer the crickets to your anoles the next day. Some stores make an effort and nutrient boost insects as a standard feeding procedure. Inquire as to the diet a store feeds its insect prey. Remember... Every time a lizard eats it also ingests the gut contents of its prey. A lizard is what its prey eats.

MULTIVITAMIN/MINERAL SUPPLEMENTATION

Every other feeding (twice a week), insects fed to green anoles must be supplemented with a quality reptile or bird vitamin/mineral powder. This is done by adding a small amount of the powder in a jar, introducing the crickets, gently shaking the jar to coat the crickets with the mix and introducing them in a feeding dish in the vivarium. A feeding dish such as a small porcelain dish is recommended to prevent rapid dispersal of the crickets and the subsequent loss of vitamin/mineral coating.

FEEDING SCHEDULE

On an optimal feeding schedule, green anoles should be offered food every other day. Do not offer more crickets or food items than the lizards will eat at a sitting. Usually, two to three appropriately sized food items are all that is required for an anole to have its fill. Excess crickets simply dropped in a vivarium rapidly lose all vitamin/mineral coating. These loose insects will be eaten later as the anoles become hungry again. When you feed them next time, they will not be as eager to feed on newly introduced food (they will be full from having eaten the stragglers) and a pattern of delayed feeding on unsupplemented crickets will occur. The end result can be vitamin deficient lizards, so don't feed more than your lizards will eat at a sitting.

WATER

Anoles do not readily drink from a bowl containing still water. They drink most readily from droplets of water which reflect light. The easiest and most recommended method for providing water to anoles is to lightly spray their enclosures once to twice daily during the daytime. They will then lap droplets from leaves and the glass sides of the vivarium. Purified bottled water is recommended for this purpose or accumulations of minerals will quickly stain the glass of your vivarium and impair viewing. Other methods used include placing a shallow container of water in which a section of aquarium tubing connected to an air pump has been placed. The bubbling water will create the light play that anoles use to recognize water. There is also an effective and simple passive drip system that can be used which consists of placing a low deli container under an area with overhanging leaves inside the vivarium. Another deli container with a tiny hole at the bottom is placed outside of the vivarium on the area of the screen top just above the underlying container. Fill the upper container with water and it will drip water slowly one drop at a time, with drops striking the underlying leaves before landing in the lower container. The anoles will drink from splattered droplets on the leaves.

The Hispaniolan giant anole (*Anolis ricordi*). This impressive species was once imported in small numbers from Haiti. Photo by John Tashjian.

Anolis occulatus from Rosean Dominica. Photo by John Tashjian.

The Cuban anole. This is the largest of the anoles as well as one of the longest lived. These impressive lizards will adapt readily to captivity if provided with a large enclosure, heat and humidity. With some regular handling, some individuals become quite tame. Photo by Chris Estep.

Anolis smallwoodi palardis, a very attractive giant anole. This specimen originated from Guantanamo Bay, Cuba. Photo by John Tashjian.

HANDLING

Though there is a small anole harness sometimes offered in the pet trade, anoles for the most part are small and at times flighty lizards that are best observed rather than taken out and handled. If you want a pet lizard that can occasionally be taken out and handled, consider an Australian bearded dragon (*Pogona vitticeps*) or blue-tongue skink (*Tiliqua scincoides*). Both of these species are now bred in some numbers in the U.S. Leopard geckos (*Eublepharis macularius*) which are relatively inexpensive compared to the aforementioned species will also be much more suitable for handling than green anoles. Green iguanas that are tame can also be handled as can a number of other medium to large lizards such as Sudan plated lizards (*Gerrhosaurus major*).

An Australian bearded dragon (*Pogona vitticeps*). This is one of the very best of all the "pet" lizards. Fortunately, increasing numbers are now regularly bred in the United States. Photo by Robert Mailloux.

Diseases and Disorders

Partially because of their small size, green anoles are difficult to treat and, as a general rule, like most small lizards, they will usually die once they appear ill. The low cost of green anoles and their relative abundance have resulted in the lack of veterinary treatment of these animals when they are ill. The veterinary treatment of such small lizards would cost many times the initial price of the animals and is frequently unsuccessful. Indeed, the particular and rapid metabolism of small lizards often results in rapid decline when ill. The small size also makes the dosage and administration of medication difficult for herpetoculturists. Furthermore, the rapid rate of decline of small lizards seldom allows enough time for the medication to take effect. Thus, careful daily monitoring of small reptiles is important to notice when their condition appears even slightly off. Efforts should be made to determine early on any possible diseases or environmental causes.

Botflies: Parasitism by botfly larvae is a common cause of death of green anoles in the wild. Sometimes green anoles purchased from stores will die as a result of botfly parasitism. The adult botfly will lay eggs under the skin of an anole. After the eggs hatch, the maggots will feed on the inside of the anole. Typically, one day an anole will have an open sore from which one or more botfly maggots will be visible. These animals should be euthanized by placing them in a plastic deli cup with cover and putting the cup in the freezer. Anoles parasitized with botfly larvae seldom survive.

Other internal parasites: These should not be of much concern to herpetoculturists unless their animals are eating yet failing to gain or maintain weight. A fecal sample can be taken by a veterinarian if necessary. Administering wormers to green anoles may be problematical in group situations, i. e. a newly imported group of anoles at a retail dealer. One method consists of placing all the anoles in a box. Weight the box full of anoles, then weight the box by itself and subtract the weight of the anoles which will give the weight of the anole group. Then, tablets of a wormer such as piperazine are weighed to treat the entire group. They are then pulverized finely with a mortar and pestle. At the next feeding small crickets are placed in a container with the pulverized wormer, shaken to be coated with the wormer and fed to the group. The treatment should be repeated three times (once every 7-10 days). Other medications can be administered to anole groups or groups of other small lizards in this manner. Flagyl® (metronidazole) in pulverized form can be effectively administered to a group in the same manner for treatment of flagellate protozoans.

A female green anole will use its snout to bury an exposed egg by creating a depression underneath it. Photo by Chris Estep.

Anolis ferreus from Marie Gallante, Lesser Antilles. Many of the more attractive and difficult to obtain anoles are worth breeding in captivity. Photo by Tom Jones.

A pair of green anoles mating. Photo Chris Estep.

"Blue" morph of the green anole. This attractive color morph is highly sought by collectors and warrants captive propagation. Photo by Chris Estep.

Respiratory infections: In anoles, a puffed up appearance of the body and occasional gaping followed by forced exhalations are characteristic symptoms of respiratory infections. Other associated symptoms include listlessness and loss of appetite.

Treatment: Increase cage temperature to 85°F-88°F with no drop at night.

Administering of antibiotics through a nebulizer can be useful when treating groups of animals. Other methods used by some herpetoculturists to treat groups of anoles include pulverizing an antibiotic such as tetracycline with a mortar and pestle and coating the food with the powder. Another method is to put an oral antibiotic in the water when misting. A veterinarian should be consulted to obtain the most effective antibiotic and to determine dosage when administering to a group of animals.

Gastroenteritis:
Typical symptoms include runny stools, caked and /or smeared diarrhea around the vent area, loss of appetite, loss of weight and listlessness. The only way to reliably diagnose the cause is to have a stool check performed by a veterinarian. Most people will not bother because of the cost. Some herpetoculturists will routinely treat these animals by administering Flagyl® (metronidazole) at a dosage of 75 mg/kg (0.075mg/g). This will treat animals with flagellate protozoans, a common cause of gastroenteritis in reptiles. In group situations, Flagyl® can be finely pulverized and used to coat crickets or other insect food items. The treatment should be repeated in two weeks.

Though some of the above methods for treating small reptiles may seem unprofessional and haphazard to veterinarians, essentially a "shotgun approach", the fact is that they are an effective method for treating small lizards particularly when the cost of a lizard and the probable high mortality risk do not justify the costs of veterinary treatment.

Anoles often adopt a mottled darkened coloration when they are dying.

Breeding

Because of their low cost and their relative abundance, herpetoculturists will make no concerned efforts to breed green anoles, though they will make efforts at propagating some of the more exotic and difficult to obtain *Anolis* species.

Nonetheless, when properly maintained, green anoles will breed readily in a vivarium. For many herpetoculturists, this is first apparent when a hatchling anole is one day seen moving about the vivarium.

To induce breeding in green anoles, the photoperiod during the winter should be reduced to 10 hours of daylight and 14 hours of darkness for two months. At night, the temperature should be allowed to drop to as low as 60°F although green anoles will tolerate temperatures into the 40's for brief periods without harm. The daytime temperature during this cooling period should be a few degrees cooler. Anoles will not feed as much or as readily during this cool period. If other tropical companion animals are kept in the vivarium, the minimum nighttime temperature should be 65°F with 68°F-72°F being the more desirable temperature range and the daytime temperatures should be allowed to go up to standard normal range (low to mid 80's) during the daylight hours.

Breeding activity will usually be seen in the spring, but may extend into summer. Green anoles typically lay multiple clutches of single eggs as often as every two weeks. Anoles in general will seek to lay their eggs under a piece of wood or will bury them in a shallow depression in the ground.

If you are interested in raising anoles from eggs, the eggs should be removed and placed in an incubating container. Eggs allowed to remain in the vivarium where adults are maintained can result in hatchlings being eaten by the adults or other vivarium animals soon after emergence from the eggs.

INCUBATION

Because of the low cost of most anoles, few individuals will be willing to spend the money on designing an incubator for hatching anole eggs. An inexpensive method is to remove the eggs and bury them in a layer of moistened vermiculite (barely moist, specifically half vermiculite and half water by weight which will be approximately one part water to twelve to fourteen parts vermiculite by volume) inside a small food storage container or deli container. The eggs should be buried just beneath the surface of the vermiculite. The container should be covered and a few holes punched into the cover to allow for some aeration. The container should then be placed inside the vivarium away from direct exposure to heat lamps or subsurface heat. Under these conditions, green anole eggs will usually hatch in 35-40 days at a temperature of 84°F-86°F (29°C-30°C).

Jamaican giant anole (*Anolis garmani*). Photo by Jim Bridges©.

Anole Vivaria as Community Vivaria

One of the advantages of keeping smaller lizards is that if one has a large vivarium, other species of reptiles and/or amphibians can often be housed and displayed in the same enclosure. The general rule is to only keep together animals which are more or less of the same size and, to the best of one's judgment, not capable of harming or eating each other. This allows for the design of unusually interesting vivaria as fascinating as community tropical fish aquaria.

PREREQUISITES FOR ESTABLISHING A COMMUNITY VIVARIUM

A key to designing a successful community vivarium is to landscape the vivarium to stratify the space into a diversity of niches. Choosing animal species which will not compete for the same vivarium niches will also be critical. For example , one can combine semiterrestrial and arboreal anoles, small geckos which will tend to remain on the inner walls of the vivarium or vertical slabs of cork bark, tree frogs that will only tend to become active towards evening and one or two tiny species of toad or possibly small terrestrial lizards. There will have to be considerable experimentation and careful monitoring in the initial set up of a community vivarium. As with fish, you will have to be careful not to overcrowd. The following are essential prerequisites to combining animals in a community vivarium.

1) Prior to introducing any new animal to the community vivarium, the new animal(s) should be quarantined and maintained in a smaller vivarium for at least thirty days. During the quarantine period, observe the health status of the animal. Is it active? Does it feed readily? Is it gaining or losing weight? Is it gaping? Any health problems should be treated. An animal should be active, feeding well and with good weight prior to introduction into a community vivarium. A particular concern of all herpetoculturists is the introduction of life-threatening viral diseases. Though this may be nearly impossible to completely avoid, quarantining animals for at least thirty days and preferably sixty days will minimize the risk of introducing such diseases.

2) When possible, treat the animals for parasites during the quarantine period. In a closed system such as a vivarium, parasites with direct life cycles can increase to critical levels and eventually wipe out inhabitants of a community vivarium. In addition, certain species may be particularly susceptible to parasites of another species. Treating parasites may be easier said than done but a good reptile veterinarian should be able to help you establish both a diagnostic and treatment protocol. In time, with a basic microscope and a small amount of equipment, you

should be able to identify and treat some of the more common parasites. (**Advanced Vivarium Systems** is publishing an essential manual on reptile parasites and their treatment, *Understanding Reptile Parasites* by Robert Klingenberg which will become available in September 1992)

3) Only mix amphibians and reptiles with a snout to vent length at least 50% of the snout to vent length of the largest animal. These are broad guidelines.

4) Don't overcrowd. A rule of thumb for a community vivarium is that the vivarium should have a length at least five times the total length of the largest animal and a width at least one and a half times the total length of the largest animal. Another rule of thumb is that the sum of the total lengths of all the animals in the vivarium should not exceed three fourths of the length of the vivarium. This is a broad guideline that can be somewhat exceeded in wide vivaria or if one combines animals that inhabit different niches in the vivarium i.e. geckos on the walls, anoles on branches and small toads or terrestrial lizards at ground level.

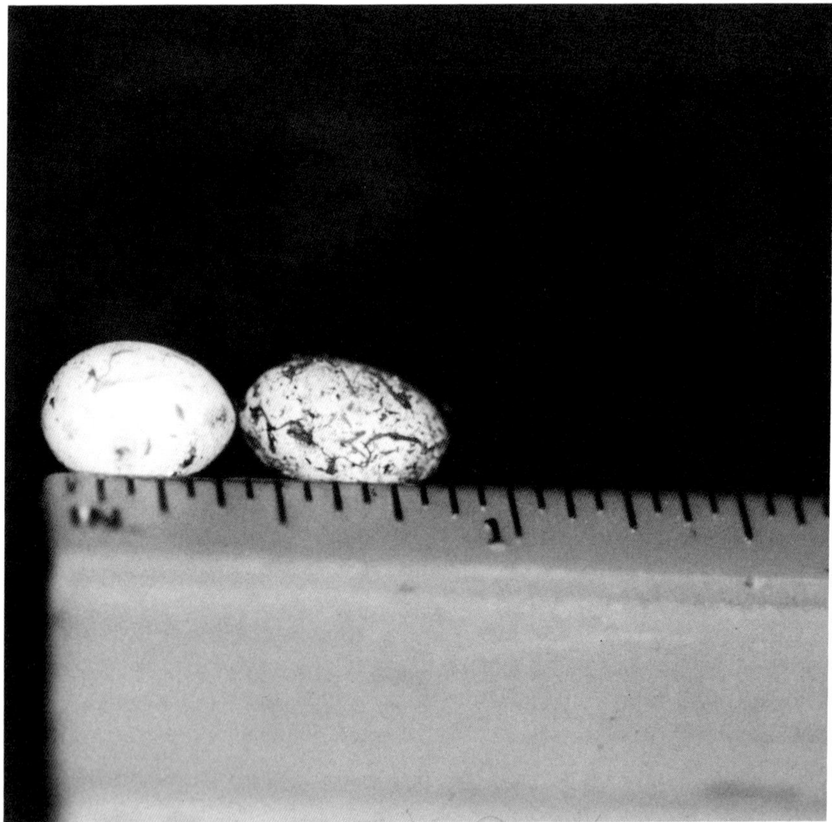

Eggs of the green anole (*Anolis carolinensis*). This species will readily breed in a home vivarium if the photoperiod is properly adjusted.

Notes on Other Anoles

At the time of writing, relatively few anole species are offered in the pet trade other than species which can be collected in the U.S. The following are usually available during the warmer months.

BROWN ANOLE (*Anolis sagrei)*

This was one of the first introduced anoles to become established in south Florida. The brown anole is more terrestrial than the green anole and prefers larger resting areas i.e bases of tree trunks. In a well designed vivarium, these lizards will make an attractive display particularly the males with their large orange-red dewlaps. With adequate food, one or more brown anoles can be maintained with a small group of green anoles. Efforts must be made to select animals within the size range of the green anoles one is maintaining. A large male brown anole can find a small green anole a tasty morsel.

Size: Large males can reach a total length of 8 1/2 inches.

Sexing: Males larger than females, males have larger heads and when excited raise a slight nuchal crest. Males have beautiful bright orange red dewlaps with a light edge.

Breeding: Similar to green anoles, but night temperatures during the cooling period should not drop below 60°F.

BIG HEADED ANOLES (*Anolis cybotes*)

This species used to be imported in some numbers from Haiti. Today they are mostly available in small numbers as collected specimens from limited areas of south Florida where they have been introduced.

Their appeal is the relatively short but large head of males. The males also have stout bodies with generally heftier proportions than found in most anoles. In habits, they are a bit like *A. sagrei.*

Size: Males up to 8 inches. Females are considerably smaller typically around 5 inches.

Sexing: Males are larger, have proportionately larger heads and a large pale yellow dewlap.

Breeding: Like *A. sagrei,* but minimum night temperature should be 65°F.

CUBAN OR KNIGHT ANOLE (*Anolis equestris*)

This is one of the largest of the anoles. It cannot be kept with green anoles or any smaller lizard. This species which has been introduced and established in southern Florida is one of the outstanding anoles. They are impressive, display well and with a minimum of care will thrive in vivaria and will reproduce with some regularity. With some handling young established specimens can become relatively tame though it should be made clear that these lizards are capable of inflicting a nasty bite. They are best kept in groups of one male to one or more females. Knight anoles will eat larger prey including smaller lizards. In captivity, they will readily feed on large crickets, king mealworms and pink to early stage fuzzy mice.

Size: Large males can reach a total length of 20 inches.

Sexing: Males will grow to a larger size than females. The head of males, particularly in older males, is significantly more massive and its upper surface is more rugose than that of females. Hemipenile bulges at the base of tail are the best indicators of sex.

Longevity: In captivity, Cuban anoles can live up to ten years or more.

Minimum vivarium size: A standard 29 gallon (30"L X 18"H X 12"W) aquarium with screen top. For a breeding group of one male and two females, at least a 55 gallon vivarium is recommended. Only larger vivarium sizes will allow for naturalistic vivarium design. This species can also successfully be kept loose on houseplants and branches set in a corner of a room with spotlights for heat and light.

Vivarium design: Add thicker branches both diagonally and vertically. Use larger plants such as Monstera (cut-leaf philodendron),Ficus species and large philodendron species. Dracaena can be planted sideways to provide room for climbing.

Diet: Hatchlings same as adult green anoles. Adult cuban anoles will feed on adult crickets, king mealworms and pink mice. The author has observed knight anoles kept with a green iguana feed on plant matter particularly ripe tomatoes.

Breeding: With decreased photoperiod in the winter and night temperature drops to 68°F, knight anoles will breed readily. Females usually lay up to four clutches of 1-2 eggs. Hatchlings are very attractive with white bars on the sides. Initially hatchlings may be reluctant to feed and may have to be hand fed prekilled insects the first few feedings. Hatchlings tend to be delicate and should be maintained under optimal conditions.

Compatible species: One problem with knight anoles is that they will try to eat whatever moves and could possibly fit in their mouths so any cage mates must be of similar or slightly greater size. Another problem is that if annoyed, they will

A green anole (top) and an Asian golden treefrog (*Rhacophorus leucomystax*) resting on an Epidendrum orchid. Photo by Vern French.

readily bite and possibly cause injury to a cage mate. They are compatible with some species of equal or greater size, i.e. green iguanas if kept in very large vivaria.

JAMAICAN ANOLE (*Anolis garmani*)

This moderately large species has been recently introduced in south Florida and is now regularly offered by specialist dealers.

The Jamaican anole is a very attractive but also very nervous, aggressive and territorial anole. They are best kept in large well planted vivaria. Keep only one male per enclosure with up to three females. Their aggressive and secretive nature limits their appeal but in time they will come out of hiding. This species is definitely not recommended for handling.

Size: Males up to 14 inches.

Sexing: Males are larger than females with larger heads and hemipenile bulges.

They can be maintained like the Cuban anole but are best kept by themselves in single species vivaria.

OTHER ANOLES

Other *Anolis* species are occasionally available in the pet trade in small numbers. Recently *Anolis* from Guyanas and crested anoles *Anolis cristatellus* from Puerto Rico have become available. Anoles from Nicaragua have also been sporadically imported. There are rumors of some of the other Cuban species becoming one day available (Cuba has some outstanding larger species). As a rule most *Anolis* species can be maintained under the general guidelines mentioned in this book except that they will usually not be as tolerant of cool night temperatures or winter temperatures as the green anole. Careful observation of the behavior of anoles should clue you as to their requirements i.e. whether they bask or appear to avoid heat, whether they drink unusually large amounts of water, the preferred vivarium niche, their territorial or aggressive behaviors. A good herpetoculturist is invariably a good observer and one who can adjust the captive environment to meet an animal's essential needs.

COMPATIBLE ANIMALS

OTHER ANIMALS FOR ANOLE VIVARIA

The following are some species which can be kept with adult green anoles (juveniles will be eaten by anything that can swallow them), particularly in larger well designed vivaria (29 gallons and up) and planted vivaria with a variety of vertical and horizontal shelters.

Asian long tailed lizard (*Takydromus sexlineatus*). These interesting lacertids will fare well with green anoles in large vivaria. Unfortunately, imports harbor internal parasites which must be treated.

Two male anoles performing aggressive displays. Most anoles are highly territorial and should be carefully monitored when maintained in groups. Photo by Vern French.

GECKOS

Several small gecko species can be successfully maintained with green anoles. The following are some of the species that are compatible.

HOUSE GECKOS (*Hemidactylus sp.*). SE. Asia.

These will fare well with green anoles as long as sharp drops in night temperature are avoided. Minimum night temperature should be 65°F.

Size: 2 1/2 - 3 1/2 inches for most species.

Sexing: Males have visible hemipenile bulges at the base of the tail.

Diet: Similar to green anoles.

Breeding : House geckos will breed readily and lay multiple clutches of 2 eggs each

FLYING GECKOS (*Ptychozoon lionatum* and other species). SE. Asia.

These neat medium sized geckos will fare well with anoles only under a situation of keeping smaller flying geckos with larger green anoles or medium sized species of anoles. Given an opportunity, larger flying geckos will find smaller anoles a large but all and all satisfying meal.

Size: Up to 6 1/2 inches

Sexing: Males have pronounced hemipenile bulges at the base of the tail that females lack.

Breeding: Flying geckos will breed readily in vivaria laying multiple clutches of two eggs each.

GOLD DUST DAY GECKOS (*Phelsuma laticauda*)

These beautiful diurnal geckos from Madagascar should be kept in single pairs or trios unless a very large vivarium is provided.

Several other small day geckos such as peacock day geckos (*P. quadriocellata*) and leaf-tail d.g. *(P. serraticauda)* will fare well with anoles but only one species should be selected and only single pairs or trios. In addition to the standard insect fare, once a week , day geckos should be given banana baby food with calcium carbonate or a reptile calcium/D3 supplement. This mix should be offered in a small shallow container (such as a jar lid) placed on the ground against the wall

Spring peeper (*Hyla crucifer*), one of several small North American treefrogs which will fare well in anole vivaria. The plant is a jewel orchid (*Haemaria discolor*). Both the plant and the frog have been long term residents in one of the large vivaria pictured earlier. Photo by Vern French.

Gray tree frog (*Hyla versicolor*) resting on the leaves of an Epidendrum orchid photographed in the same vivarium as the previous tree frog. Photo by Vern French.

of a vivarium. If maintained properly, the above day geckos will breed readily, laying multiple clutches of two eggs each.

PIGMY SKINKS (*Mabouia macularia*). SE. Asia.

Size: Up to 3 1/4 inches

Sexing: Mature males are more colorful with orange on the underside of the throat but this is not always reliable particularly in younger males. A sure fire method is to evert the hemipenes which is easily done by holding a skink upside down in one hand while pulling back the anal plate with the thumb and with the other hand using the thumb beginning at an area roughly 1/2-1/3 of an inch from the vent, pressing in and up toward the vent. This should be done gently. Little pressure is required to cause hemipenile eversion in males.

These small attractive skinks are good companions to anoles only in a large vivarium that does not house too many animals. They do not like excessively warm temperatures but do well at temperatures in the mid to upper 70's. Generally, they should be kept like long tailed grass lizards (see below) with which they can be readily maintained. These pretty skinks are hardy, interesting little animals which tend to be secretive, frequently spending their time in shelters or burrowed in fine orchid bark which is recommended as a ground medium. The diet should consist of two to three week old crickets, though these skinks will feed on dead crushed larger insects.

ASIAN LONG-TAILED LIZARDS, ALSO CALLED ASIAN GRASS LIZARDS (*Takydromus sexlineatus*)

Size: Up to 13 inches total length with a snout to vent length just under three inches.

Sexing: The tails of males thicken past the vent and are generally markedly thicker compared to the more tapered tails of females. The difference is unmistakable. Mature males also tend to have somewhat brighter, higher contrast coloration with the background color often a darker, richer shade than that of females. The lateral stripes are cream yellow compared to the off-white of females.

These elongated slender lizards of the family Lacertidae are suitable companion lizards in green anole vivaria that are not kept too warm. In the author's experience these lizards do well at temperatures in the mid 70's to 82°F. This species lives primarily in grasslands and requires a moderately high relative humidity like anoles. However, they will not fare well in vivaria with saturated humidity and poor ventilation. A layer one inch thick or more of orchid bark is recommended as a ground medium. This will provide these lizards with a burrowing medium they seem to enjoy and may possibly require. A small humidifying shelter is recommended. As a primary diet, two to three week old crickets are a must because this species will only consume smaller insects. They will, however, feed to some degree on crushed up prekilled larger insects. A small shallow water dish should be provided. If you look at them closely, these lizards have neat little faces with intense eyes. They're interesting vivarium lizards if you can get them established. Long-tailed lizards are egg-layers laying from four to ten tiny eggs per clutch. Under proper conditions they will lay several clutches per year.

Species compatibility: Long-tailed grass lizards can only be kept with small companion animals. Even a large flying gecko may find a smaller long-tailed lizard a tasty treat. Lots of herps will consider them a snack and so will birds. Think before you mix.

Breeding: Pre-breeding conditioning is similar to green anoles but the night temperature should not be lower than 65°F.

Diseases and disorders: Some of the groups of imports have poor survival rates. If one excludes poor husbandry as a causal factor, flagellate protozoans can be a common cause of decline. In many imported lizards, the unsanitary watering methods are a primary cause of disease spread.

GREEN TREE FROG (*Hyla cinerea*). U.S.A.

This pretty and readily available U.S. species will fare well in larger (20 gallon plus) uncrowded vivarium containing anoles.

The only additional requirement is a water dish with a rock in it to allow for easy access in and out of the container. Purified water or a high quality drinking water should be used. Clean water should be available at all times.

Other tree frogs and toads

Spring peepers (*Hyla crucifer*) and gray tree frogs (*Hyla versicolor*) have also been successfully maintained in vivaria with anoles. Many other small species of tree frogs would probably also fare well. If the vivarium is very large, miniature species of toads could probably also be included. A shallow container of water which must be kept clean should be available at all times.

Diet: Similar to anoles

A male green anole eating the shed skin off its toes. This picture is also proof that green anoles don't mimick the coloration of their surroundings.

Anolis luteogularis, another giant anole from Cuba. Photo by John Tashjian.

A captive born and raised *Anolis nebulosa* from Sonora, Mexico, courtesy of the Arizona Sonoran Desert Museum. Photo by John Tashjian.

Martinique spotted anole *(Anolis roquet sumus)* displaying its dewlap. Photo by Jim Bridges©.

Conclusion

This booklet has presented in a very general and limited manner the possibilities of designing naturalistic community vivaria for amphibians and reptiles. There are many other landscape designs possible as well as many other species of amphibians and reptiles that would fare well under these conditions. Future works by the author will elaborate on designing naturalistic vivaria and on keeping mixed communities of amphibians and reptiles. Nonetheless one should be open to experimentation in this area as long as certain basic criteria are met:

1) A large vivarium. The larger it is, the greater the opportunities of successfully keeping several species together.

2) Select small species. Larger species will damage the landscape, require more space and will defecate too frequently and in too copious amounts to keep a naturalistic vivarium going for very long.

3) Quarantine and treat animals prior to introduction.

4) Keep species together that have more or less similar environmental requirements.

5) Don't overcrowd.

6) Put as much focus on the plants as on the animals. Well planted and designed vivaria enhance the beauty of the animals.

7) Monitor animals and plants daily.

8) Don't hesitate to make changes, particularly when various elements of a vivarium are not working.

Recommended Reading

1. De Vosjoli P. 1990. *The Right Way to Feed Insect Eating Lizards,* Advanced Vivarium Systems. Lakeside, CA.

2. Schwartz A. and R.W. Henderson. 1985. *A Guide to the Identification of the Amphibians and Reptiles of the West Indies Exclusive of Hispaniola.* Milwaukee Public Museum.

Note: This is a user friendly, illustrated guide to the herpetofauna of the West Indies. A great tool for identifying anoles.

3. Wilson D.W. and Louis Porras. 1983. *The Ecological Impact of Man on the South Florida Herpetofauna.* University of Kansas Publications. Museum of Natural History.

4. Zimmerman, Elke. 1986. *Breeding Terrarium Animals.* T.F.H.

This is one of the best references for keeping a variety of vivarium animals. A must have for any serious vivarist.

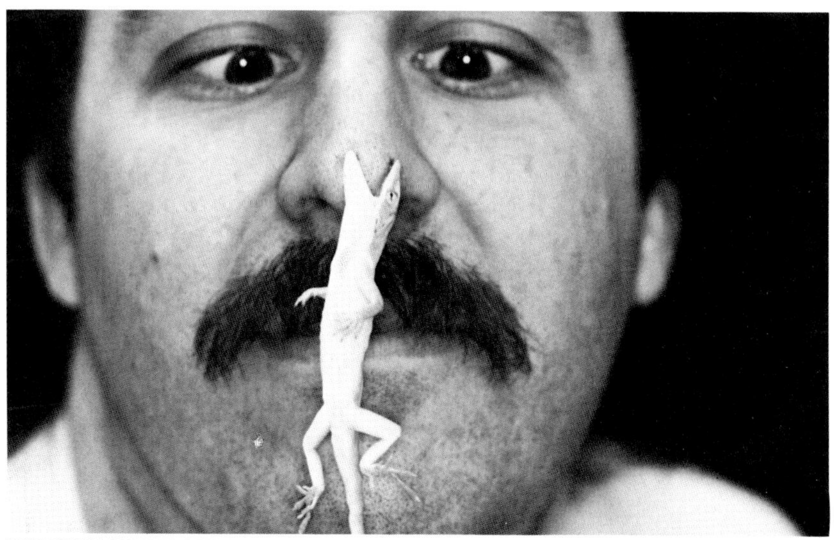

REVENGE OF THE GREEN ANOLE!
Even though this is a picture that the tabloids would pay dearly for, this is a good example of what not to do with anoles. The infamous man in the picture ended up with scabs on his nose. This type of humor can be harmful to both man and beast. Nonetheless, an enlarged copy of this in the office is bound to elicit a chuckle.

Prehensile tailed polychrus (*Polychrus marmoratus*). This interesting lizard is occasionally imported from the Guyanas. In the author's experience, this species must be treated for parasites to establish in captivity. High relative humidity and good ventilation will also be required. Photo by Jim Bridges©.

A male Martinique anole (*Anolis roquet roguet)*. Many of the more attractive anoles originate from the West Indies. Photo by Jim Bridges.